GOD'S AGENDA PAST, PRESENT, AND FUTURE

What's in Your Box?

God Wants You Back

By:

William C. Edmondson

PROISLE PUBLISHING

God's Agenda

Past, Present, and Future

To order additional copies of this book, contact:

Proisle Publishing Services LLC

1177 6th. Ave 5th floor

New York, NY 10036 USA

Phone: (+1 347-922-3779)

Info@proislepublishing.com

Table of Contents

Preface...4

Chapter 1: Reflections on the Bible 6

Chapter 2: So You Say There is no Good?....................8

CHAPTER 3: In the Beginning 10

Chapter 4: Time Begins...13

Chapter 5: The Angelic Realm 15

Chapter 6: Why Did Lucifer Rebel?.............................17

Chapter 7: Why Did God Create Earth?.....................20

Chapter 8: What Is Man? 23

Chapter 9: Why Did God Create Man?........................24

Chapter 10: Adam and Eve Died...................................30

Chapter 11: The Results of Lucifer's Decision...........35

Chapter 12: God's for Mankind's Plan Redemption.............38

Chapter 13: The Comfort Zone 44

Chapter 14: Who Rules Your Box?................................51

Chapter 15: The Box—Heart or Comfort Zone 59

Chapter 16: Abraham..61

Chapter 17: Isaac and Jacob..65

Chapter 18: The Pillar of Cloud and the Pillar of Fire 70

Chapter 19: The Promised Land.....................................71

Chapter 20: God Commissioned Joshua.......................72

Chapter 21: Job's Box..76

Chapter 22: Saul...80

Chapter 23: Get Out of the Box 83

Chapter 24: What Have We Learned?............................85

Chapter 25: Accepting Christ...89

Appendix 1: Why I Believe in the God of the Bible.............92

Appendix 2: Can We Trust the Bible? 97

Preface

It was an ordinary Bible study you might say, but it seemed to me that I always got something beneficial out of Bible study. I can't tell you how the study started or what the subject was, only that it evolved to focus on the will of God. It didn't seem to be impressive enough that I thought much more about it until about two or three nights later.

I awoke in the middle of the night and was wide awake with the will of God on my mind. I couldn't get back to sleep due to the many thoughts racing through my mind. I felt that God wanted to tell me something. So I got up, went to where I do my devotions, took a tablet and pen, and began to write what was coming into my mind about the will of God. I wrote rapidly to catch these thoughts for about an hour and a half, and then He seemed to release me to go back to bed.

For the next couple of months as I was doing devotions, God would show me thoughts about His will; I couldn't read the Bible or a book without God saying to me, "This is what I'm trying to tell you." And then the thoughts seemed to subside significantly. So I guessed it was time to organize my thoughts and write them in an orderly fashion resulting in this book.

In His infinite wisdom, God gave us the Bible, His written Word penned by men He chose to record what He wanted us to know. His truth is hiding in the Bible, and it is revealed only by the intense study of its contents. Reading the Bible many times begins to unlock those hidden truths about how God dealt with man after he fell out of his original relationship with his Creator. The gift that caused his fall—his ability to make decisions for himself—is the gift he must use for his redemption. He chose to rebel against God, so he now has to choose to accept God's plan for his redemption or suffer the everlasting consequences of his decision. I feel God's ultimate plan goes far beyond the defeat of Satan.

In 1 John 1:5–10, we read a summary of what God wants us to know.

> This is the message we have heard from him and proclaim to you, that God is light, and in him is no darkness at all. If we say we have fellowship with him while we walk in darkness, we lie and do not practice the truth.
>
> But if we walk in the light, as he is in the light, we have fellowship with one another, and the blood of Jesus his Son cleanses us from all sin. If we say we have no sin, we deceive ourselves, and the truth is not in us. If we confess our sins, he is faithful and just to forgive us our sins and to cleanse us from all unrighteousness. If we say we have not sinned, we make him a liar, and his word is not in us.

Whether you are a Christian or an unbeliever, I believe you will find this book beneficial to your understanding of how your box works and why it is there in the first place. The box, your comfort zone, that area of your being where people tell you to "get out of your box and do something". It is that area deep within you where your good or bad decisions are made and acted upon. I make no apologies for the stand I take on biblical principles as a foundation for this book, as I believe the Bible is God's message to us on how to live; therefore, I adhere to the following premises, which everyone can benefit from.

Chapter 1

Reflections on the Bible

If we are going to get out of the Bible what we need, we should agree on some points.

1. The Bible is God's Word, and not in part but in its totality. It is what God told the prophets to write. Therefore, it is His Word.

2. We can depend upon its words because they are God's words.

3. God does not lie, and He will not let His Word misrepresent Him.

4. When science and the Bible seem to disagree, accept only the proven facts of science and then investigate your understanding and interpretation of the Bible. The Bible is right, but our understanding of it might be in error. Check it out. Investigate it. The Bible is right!

5. Science has proven the universe had a beginning, and science universally agrees on the principle of cause and effect, the idea that nothing occurs without a cause. Christians agree that God was the cause, scientifically speaking, of the universe coming into being; it didn't just happen without a cause!

If we accept number 5, isn't that reason enough to accept that if God created the universe, He could dictate the text of the Bible to mankind and keep that text pure and intact?

If the Bible is God's Word,

- Shouldn't we accept it as written?
- Shouldn't we obey its sayings?
- Shouldn't we live according to it?
- Shouldn't we study it to find out what God has in store for us?
- Shouldn't we be careful not to take the scriptures out of context, for by so doing we twist its meaning to our own desires?

The Bible will speak to us if we will listen! So let us see if we can discern some things God desires for us to know.

In this book, I often refer to "man" and "mankind," but these references are not for man only, it is a reference to all mankind.

Chapter 2

So You Say There Is No God?

So you say it just happened that the universe came into being on its own?

It just happened that a million billion stars came into existence out of nothing?

It just happened that Earth was the right distance from the Sun to support life?

It just happened there is just the right amount of water and oxygen for that?

It just happened that Earth rotates every twenty-four hours to properly maintain its warmth?

It just happened that Earth's axis is tilted to give seasons?

It just happened that life came into existence on Earth?

It just happened that intelligent life appeared?

It just happened that grass is green and the sky is blue?

It just happened that bees exist to pollinate vegetation?

It just happened that people could communicate with each other?

It just happened that our heart beats sixty to seventy times a minute for seventy to eighty years without failure?

It just happened that there is order in the universe?

It just happened that the universe is fine-tuned for life?

It just happened that there is an energy source buried

deep in Earth to supply man's needs?

It just happened that man has a desire to worship?

It just happened that man has a conscience?

If all this just happened, then

- There is no purpose for life,
- There is no hope,
- There is no plan for mankind, and
- Mankind has no destiny but the grave.

If there is a God, then

- All these things just happened by God's command,
- There is a reason for life,
- There is a reason to have hope, and
- There is a destiny beyond the grave.

If there is a beginning to the universe, common sense should tell us there is a beginner, a creator.

If there is a creator, this creator is responsible for life.

If God is the reason for life, isn't it also reasonable to expect God to reveal to us the reason? Hence, we have God's holy Word, the Bible.

Nothing happens without a cause!

Chapter 3

In the Beginning

It is a rare person who has never once wondered, *where did I come from?* Not just how he or she came into existence but also where and when in the vast past did it all begin. Our minds wander over all types of things that could have happened. Our ancestors have left us with a variety of stories and myths of our beginning.

The greatest myth of all is that there is no God that we just evolved. This is a relatively recent theory brought on by Satan to deceive us. And if that is the case, the miracle of life takes on a whole new aspect. For if there is no God, the only thing that could have happened was that we just happened. We would thus have no plan, no purpose, no hope, no reason for life, and no destiny but the grave. What an awful existence that would be. The concept of having no God leaves us without hope, without a purpose for life, and just existing.

If the universe had a beginning, there must have been a beginner. In the beginning, before anything was, God existed, and He had a purpose for creating something. In the beginning, only God existed. He began His plan by creating a spirit realm to assist Him in fulfilling His plan. We humans can only imagine just what this spirit realm was like.

Over the years, science and the Bible have been at odds. The Bible declares that the heavens and earth were created by God while science often declares that there is no God and that the universe always existed. Then Edwin Hubble, working at the Mt. Wilson Observatory in California in 1929, discovered that the galaxies were moving away from one another at a very high velocity. This discovery led to the belief that the universe indeed had a beginning, which led to the big bang theory. This discovery demanded a cause as nothing happens without a cause. Christians know the cause, God, as the Bible told us over 3,500 years ago.

> In the beginning, God created the heavens and the earth. The earth was without form and void, and darkness was over the face of the deep. And the Spirit of God was hovering over the face of the waters. (Genesis 1:1–2)

If this universe had a beginning, it demands an explanation for why and how it came into existence. Science's claim is that all matter was compressed into something smaller than a pinhead.[1] Now, science admits the universe had a beginning some billions of years ago. But they still want you to believe that there is no God—that it just happened. They want you to believe

- That the universe began with a big bang that occurred about fourteen billion years ago,
- That the universe was inside a bubble that was thousands of times smaller than a pinhead,
- That it was hotter than anything imaginable,
- That this pinhead suddenly exploded and is the reason for the universe,
- That time and space began simultaneously,
- That in a fraction of a second, it grew from smaller than a pinhead to bigger than a galaxy, and
- That it is still expanding today.

---

[1] http://www.startofjourney.com/the-big-bang/.

These commonly accepted concepts cannot all be true. They are stating that there was matter to begin with—it was just super condensed. And so questions still remain: Where did this matter come from. How did it begin? The only plausible conclusion is that it did not exist in the first place. Matter had to have a beginning; God had nothing to start with, so He created it out of nothing.

Remember that before the universe existed, there was nothing, no physicality of any sort. Only the spiritual realm existed, but it did not need space or time as we know it. Time and space began when God created the universe, and they are relevant only to God's physical realm.

Chapter 4

Time Begins

Genesis 1:1 says, "In the beginning God created." With this statement, we come to realize God was placing Himself outside of and before anything that was created.

- Who is this God placing Himself before this entire physical universe came into being?
- What was He like?
- When did all this take place?
- Where is He now?
- Why did He create?
- How did He do it?

These questions need to be answered and understood. The scriptures will reveal the answers if we are willing to diligently look for them.

Let's speculate, but let us have a reasonable understanding that our speculation could be quite accurate as the Bible gives us hints.

We can only imagine what God's existence was before He began His creation of the physical universe. John 4:24 says, "God is a Spirit: and they that worship him must worship him in spirit and in truth."

We realize that God in His pre-creation existence was living in a spiritual realm. In looking back in time to the very beginning, we can understand that God's plan for something new and different from the spiritual realm was absolutely enormous. We do not know just when the angelic realm was created. Was it before or after the creation of the universe? I believe the angelic realm was in place to assist with God's plan for a new physical type of existence. This new existence would not be anything like the spiritual realm; however, it would incorporate a spiritual element. His angels would have awesome responsibilities to help shape the new realms of heaven and earth.

I can only imagine the excitement among the angels as God began His physical creation by speaking it into existence. Science calls this the big bang for lack of a better understanding of it. You see, there was nothing physical before God's creation; God created the physical realms of heaven and earth out of nothing.

Imagine everything God had to do to create this vast universe from the spiritual realm. Matter had to be created out of nothing, and the laws governing how the universe would function had to be created as well. The elements present in the universe had to be in exact proportion to one another for life to be able to exist (see appendix 1). Laws of physics, mathematics, gravity, centrifugal force, and many more needed to work with one another in order to hold everything in place, and not just dust and rocks but all the elements that make up matter. Silver and gold, oxygen, hydrogen, water, and all the elements of the periodic table (and much more) were made before life was created.

Time is relevant only to a physical realm; hence, time was created when God brought into existence the physical realm that we call the universe.

Chapter 5

The Angelic Realm

In the beginning, only God existed. He was the spirit holding all knowledge. He began His spiritual realm by creating the angels to worship Him and do His bidding. Besides worshipping God, angels minister to mankind and play an important role in meting out God's wrath as recorded in the book of Revelation.

Hebrews 1:14 asks us,

> "Are they not all ministering spirits sent out to serve for the sake of those who are to inherit salvation?"

These ministering spirits were created with varying abilities, powers, and ranks. He gave them a gift called the power of choice, the power to make decisions on their own. The power of choice was a dangerous gift as it gave His angelic creations the ability to say no to Him. Saying no to God would be to disobey Him, to sin.

Lucifer, whom we call Satan, was one of the most powerful types of angels called cherubs. He chose to disobey God and rebel with the purpose of taking over His kingdom.

Revelation 12:4 tells us that Lucifer's

> "tail swept down a third of the stars of heaven and cast them to the earth"

These *stars of heaven* are a reference to the third of the angelic realm who followed Satan in his rebellion. God knew Satan would try to intervene in His creation of humans, to whom He also gave the power of choice, free will, and to whom he would offer a plan of redemption for those who would be deceived by Satan.

Revelation 13:8 says,

> "And all that dwell upon the earth shall worship him, whose names are not written in the book of life of the Lamb slain from the foundation of the world."

This verse reveals two things. The lamb was a reference to Jesus, who paid the price of redemption by shedding His blood for the atonement of our sins, and anyone who does not worship God will worship Satan. There is no other choice—it is one or the other.

The Bible does not give us very much information concerning this angelic realm; it mentions only Michael, Gabriel, and Lucifer by name. Jewish tradition however says that there are seven arch (chief) angels. It appears that Lucifer, probably one of the three most important in the angelic realm and possibly the first angel God created, became proud of his beauty and ability and decided that he was capable of defeating God and taking over His kingdom.

Chapter 6

Why Did Lucifer Rebel?

Satan was created as a servant and was required to fulfill the duties God gave him with the intelligence God had given him. Satan used this power in an attempt to usurp God's authority and take it over as his own. His violation was a sin, which required a punishment. This punishment will one day be meted out to put away sin forever.

We do not know when or how Lucifer conceived the idea of defeating God and taking over His kingdom so he could be worshipped as the god of the universe, but it appears that he was created at or near the dawn of creation, the moment when God spoke heaven and earth into existence. The phrase *Son of the morning* in Isaiah 14:12 may indicate that Lucifer had been created when heaven and earth were created.

His rebellion may have occurred when God created man. Satan must have realized that man would be an easy target for him to conquer and use in his quest to defeat God. Regardless of when Lucifer rebelled, God knew a rebellion would occur.

Because Lucifer had been created to be a servant of the most high God, his focus should have been on that, but he turned his focus on himself; Isaiah 14:12–15 (KJV) declares,

> How art thou fallen from heaven, O Lucifer,
> *son of the morning*! how art thou cut down to
> the ground, which didst weaken the nations!
> For thou hast said in thine heart,
>
> *I will* ascend into heaven,

I *will* exalt my throne above the stars of God: *I will* sit also upon the mount of the congregation, in the sides of the north:

I will ascend above the heights of the clouds;

I will be like the most High.

Yet thou shalt be brought down to hell, to the sides of the pit. (Emphasis mine)

Satan will one day be punished for his sin by being cast into the lake of fire along with all who chose to follow him. Revelation 20:10–15 reads,

The devil who had deceived them was thrown into the lake of fire and sulfur where the beast and the false prophet were, and they will be tormented day and night forever and ever. Then I saw a great white throne and him who was seated on it. From his presence earth and sky fled away, and no place was found for them.

And I saw the dead, great and small, standing before the throne, and books were opened. Then another book was opened, which is the book of life. And the dead were judged by what was written in the books, according to what they had done. And the sea gave up the dead who were in it, Death and Hades gave up the dead who were in them, and they were judged, each one of them, according to what they had done. Then Death and Hades were thrown into the lake of fire. *This is the second death, the lake of fire.* And if anyone's name was

> not found written in the book of life, he was
> thrown into the lake of fire. (Emphasis mine)

But until that time, Satan will be the prince of this world and will create havoc in all those who have bought into his lies and have not been redeemed by the blood of the Lamb, Jesus.

Satan's ambitions have not changed since his rebellion. In fact, he seems to be pressing harder today than at any time since his first act of defiance.

In one sensc, he is completely satisfied with people simply living lives of sexual immorality and other sins. On the other hand, he seems to be dividing our nation by driving a deeper wedge between God's followers, Christians, and those who have chosen to follow Satan by their simple act of not accepting Christ. He is trying to convince the world that God is a liar and that His followers are racists, bigots, homophobes, and any other adjectives they can come up with. His efforts are intensifying as he knows his time is short.

One of his tactics to accomplish his plan has been to use people against people. God's plan was to establish a people who would choose to follow Him and do His bidding. Satan has tried over and over to destroy God's people, but his efforts have not been successful. In these last days, Satan seems to be intensifying his efforts to destroy the United dividing the country using his followers to attack and blame the Christians for all the nation's problems.

Satan expresses his disdain for God by using people to use God's name in vain. Every time a person uses cuss words it is Satan's demonic influence using people to express his hatred and contempt for God his creator.

Chapter 7

Why Did God Create Earth?

In Isaiah 45:18–25, we read that God declared Himself to be the Creator of the heavens and the earth and the reason—He created it for it to be inhabited. I believe He knew Satan would try to thwart His plans, but He created it anyway.

> For thus says the LORD, who created the heavens (he is God!), who formed the earth and made it *(he established it; he did not create it empty, he formed it to be inhabited!):* I am the LORD, and there is no other. I did not speak in secret, in a land of darkness; I did not say to the offspring of Jacob, "Seek me in vain." I the LORD speak the truth; I declare what is right. Assemble yourselves and come; draw near together, you survivors of the nations! They have no knowledge who carry about their wooden idols, and keep on praying to a god that cannot save.

> Declare and present your case; let them take counsel together! Who told this long ago? Who declared it of old? Was it not I, the LORD? And *there is no other god besides me*, a righteous God and a Savior; there is none besides me. Turn to me and be saved, all the ends of the earth! For I am God, and there is no other.

> By myself I have sworn; from my mouth has gone out in righteousness a word that shall not

> return: *To me every knee shall bow, every tongue shall swear allegiance.* Only in the LORD, it shall be said of me, are righteousness and strength; to him shall come and be ashamed all who were incensed against him. In the LORD all the offspring of Israel shall be justified and shall glory. (Emphasis mine)

Notice that God declared that He was God and that there was no other god. He also declared that every knee would bow down to Him. God created everything to be His, including us. He designed us to be his servants just as He created the angels to be whether we swear allegiance to Him or not.

He told us, "Every knee shall bow, every tongue shall swear allegiance," and this includes believers and nonbelievers. So we might ask ourselves, "Why did God do all of this, and what purpose do I have in all that He has done?" Just remember Isaiah 45:18: quoted above in verse 18: "For thus says the LORD, who created the heavens, who formed the earth and made it: I am the LORD, and there is no other." I will attempt to answer the rest of the question in the following chapters.

Science declares that space and time were created when the heavens and the earth were created. If science is right, God's realm before creation existed was outside of time and space. What was this realm like? Scientists tell us that they have evidence of at least nine dimensions existing in the universe. We in the physical realm have no idea what these dimensions were or are like, only that they exist. The physical realm has only dimensions of height, width, length, and time. We then can conclude that God and His kingdom existed in a realm of unknown characteristics.

I believe God intended to create life on other planets, but to accomplish that, He needed first to deal with Satan, his angels', and his human followers' disobedience. Sin and evil needs to be conquered before He can fulfill His plan for that.

Genesis 1:2 tells us,

> "The earth was without form and void, and darkness was over the face of the deep. And the Spirit of God was hovering over the face of the waters."

Conditions on earth needed to be changed before life could exist there. Genesis 1 gives us the order of His bringing life to exist on earth. What we are not told is His preparation of earth's natural resources—oil, gas, and minerals that man would eventually need. Life as we know it would not be pleasant without these natural resources. Oil and gas were created in the depths of the earth for mankind to use. We will not speculate on just how and when He prepared these abundant natural resources for mankind's benefit.

Chapter 8

What Is Man?

Hebrews 2:6 asks, "What is man, that thou art mindful of him?" Is man really that important to God? The answer is a resounding yes. God has revealed to us what our makeup is.

We have a physical body, and we have a soul that resides in our body that gives us our intelligence and senses. It is the soul's responsibility to make decisions for the body using the advice from the Holy Spirit or a demonic spirit. We also have a spirit given to us by God that brings life to the body and allows a relationship with God.

But as we study the Bible, we learn that there is more to man than just the body, soul, and spirit. Man was created to live forever, but when he disobeyed God, he was no longer immortal; he was alive physically but dead spiritually.

We found that we have other residents in our being affecting the choices we make. These residents are in what we call our comfort zone, our heart or box. In the beginning, the Holy Spirit was a resident of our comfort zone and provided us eternal life. But the disobedience of Adam and Eve expelled the Holy Spirit from their hearts losing their immortality. Satan immediately replaced the Holy Spirit with one of his demons. From this day forward, mankind was born with a demon as his mentor residing in his heart.

Chapter 9

Why Did God Create Man?

The first three chapters of Genesis explain what God had to say about our beginnings. The final act of God's magnificent creation was mankind, whom He created in His own image.

> Then God said, "Let us make man in our image, after our likeness. *And let them have dominion* over the fish of the sea and over the birds of the heavens and over the livestock and over all the earth and over every creeping thing that creeps on the earth." (Genesis 1:26; emphasis mine)

Being created in God's image does not mean we look like God. God is a spirit we cannot see. Because we are visible physical beings, the only way we can reflect God's image is to reflect His character.

Man was given total authority over God's creation. He was to rule over everything on earth. To do so, he received several qualities that God's other creation did not have. First was the power of choice, the ability to make his own decisions. He also gave man eternal life; his soul was to live forever; Genesis 2:7 (KJV) reads,

> "And the LORD God formed man of the dust of the ground, and breathed into his nostrils the breath of life; and man became a living soul."

He also gave them the ability to experience love, joy, peace, patience, kindness, goodness, faithfulness, gentleness, and self-control, and He gave them the power to create houses, cars, boats, televisions, phones, computers—the list goes on. In fact, we can do anything we desire through Christ; Philippians 4:13 (KJV) reads,

> "I can do all things through Christ which strengtheneth me."

According to Genesis 2:8,

> "And the LORD God planted a garden in Eden, in the east, and there he put the man whom he had formed."

In the middle of the garden were two trees of extreme importance, the tree of life and the tree of the knowledge of good and evil. God then gave two commands to Adam—he was to take care of the garden and not eat of the tree of the knowledge of good and evil.

> The LORD God took the man and put him in the garden of Eden to work it and keep it. And the LORD God commanded the man, saying, "You may surely eat of every tree of the garden, but of the tree of the knowledge of good and evil you shall not eat, for in the day that you eat of it you shall surely die." (Genesis 2:15–17)

God then allowed Adam to see all the beasts of the field

and the birds of the air and permitted him to name them all. When Adam found no one resembling him to be his helper, God caused him to sleep. He then took a rib from Adams side and created Eve to be his mate:

> "Then the man said, 'This at last is bone of my bones and flesh of my flesh; she shall be called Woman, because she was taken out of Man.'" (Genesis 2:23).

God would come in the cool of the day to the garden to commune with them and to establish a good relationship with them.

Adam and Eve faithfully carried out their responsibilities and became comfortable in their surroundings and confident in their ability to do the tasks required; they found they were able to communicate not only with God but also with all of God's creation under their control.

One day, Eve found herself alone in the beautiful garden when one of God's other creatures approached her and began a conversation about the beauty of the tree of the knowledge of good and evil. The creature was a serpent. As they were discussing this tree's beauty, the serpent said in Genesis 3:1–7,

> "Yea, hath God said, ye shall not eat of every tree of the garden?"

That was a subtle question designed to lead her astray. She responded,

> "We may eat of the fruit of the trees in the garden, but God said, 'You shall not eat of the

fruit of the tree that is in the midst of the garden, neither shall you touch it, lest you die.'"

The serpent said,

"You will not surely die. For God knows that when you eat of it your eyes will be opened, you will be like God, knowing good and evil. For God knows that when you eat of it your eyes will be opened, and you will be like God, knowing good and evil."

Was that true? She wondered. *Will eating this fruit really make me a god? What is this tree of the knowledge of good and evil? Is its fruit really deadly? Why did God allow it to be in the garden?*

So when the woman saw that the tree was good for food, and that it was a delight to the eyes, and that the tree was to be desired to make one wise, she took of its fruit and ate, and she also gave some to her husband who was with her, and he ate. Then the eyes of both were opened, and they knew that they were naked. And they sewed fig leaves together and made themselves loincloths.

She ate some of the fruit and gave some to Adam to eat. This was a decision based on a lie, a deception perpetrated on her by Satan to alienate them from God by driving a wedge between them. They died spiritually the moment they ate the fruit.

God tested their ability to obey Him because He knew that Satan would do all in his power to alienate man from his Creator. The tree was not evil, and its fruit was not deadly; the tree was used only for the test. Would man obey God and refuse to eat, or would he succumb to the deception Satan would perpetrate on them? The fruit of this tree did not cause them to lose their immortality; disobeying God did that. Sin causes a separation from God. Physically, they were still alive, but spiritually, they instantly died.

In his war with God, Satan deceived Eve and convinced her to disobey God's command and bring Adam along with her disobedience. Instead of being God's servants, they became Satan's slaves as did all their descendants.

God had known that Satan would meddle in His creation of mankind and that mankind would not be unable to withstand the lies that Satan would use to enslave them. God, however, had a plan from the beginning of creation to purchase back mankind from that slavery.

The angels that rebelled had exercised their freedom of choice, but God had no plans to redeem the fallen angels. Their only hope was to defeat God and take over His kingdom; otherwise, they would end up in the lake of fire forever. Their plan was to drag mankind into their battle with God. Matthew 25:41 reads,

> Then he will say to those on his left, "Depart from me, you cursed, into the eternal fire prepared for the devil and his angels."

This eternal fire is also known as the lake of fire and had been prepared only for the devil and his angels. So if God had created man with a plan for redemption, why would he not take advantage of God's plan? God knew this when He created man, so He created a plan of redemption for mankind. Satan used man's free will to make man a pawn in his battle against God, and God's plan was to use man's free will to shake off Satan's shackles.

God's plan to make this escape possible required that a price had to be paid— the blood of a perfect, sinless individual needed to be sacrificed for their redemption. No mere man, however, could satisfy that requirement; as Romans 3:23 says,

> "for all have sinned and fall short of the
> glory of God."

So God's plan was that His Son would be born through a virgin without a man's involvement and thus be born sinless. Jesus, the Son of God, lived a sinless life for the purpose of satisfying the requirement of mankind's redemption. John the Baptist tells us in John 1:29,

> "Behold, the Lamb of God, who takes away
> the sin of the world!"

Satan is not your friend; he just wants to use you as he used Adam and Eve in his fight to defeat God and take over His kingdom. Through deceit, he stole mankind's right to rule the earth. By stealing that right, he put you under his control. You were born a slave to Satan. Your only hope is to return to Jesus and accept Him as your Redeemer who will welcome you back into a righteous fellowship with Him. He paid the price for your redemption, why not accept Him?

Chapter 10

Adam and Eve Died

After they ate the fruit, Adam and Eve suddenly realized they were naked, so they hid among the trees when they heard God approaching. They had not died, had God lied to them as the serpent seemed to indicate, or had they just not understood? Something happened, but what? Were they still going to die? Could eating the fruit of this tree actually cause death? What was God really going to do? Physically they were still alive, but spiritually they had died.

Adam and Eve were banished from the garden for their disobedience, and that would cause their children to be born spiritually dead. They lost access to the tree of life, and regaining access to it would require spiritual rebirth.

We read in Genesis that God had created man to do two things—populate the earth and take care of it. But I think God also wanted them to take part in His battle against Satan and help throw him into the lake of fire so that phase two of God's plan could be implemented. We can only speculate about what God's plan was once Satan was defeated, but 1 Corinthians 2:9 reads,

> "But, as it is written, 'What no eye has seen, nor ear heard, nor the heart of man imagined, what God has prepared for those who love him.'"

God has something prepared for you, but you must return to be His servant by accepting Christ as your Redeemer. We see in Revelation 5:10 where we will be kings and priests on earth:

"And hast made us unto our God kings and priests: and we shall reign on the earth."

But what does He have planned for us in the rest of the universe?

Revelation 20:1–3 and 7–10 tell us,

Then I saw an angel coming down from heaven, holding in his hand the key to the bottomless pit and a great chain. And he seized the dragon, that ancient serpent, who is the devil and Satan, and bound him for a thousand years, and threw him into the pit, and shut it and sealed it over him, so that he might not deceive the nations any longer, until the thousand years were ended. After that he must be released for a little while …

And when the thousand years are ended, Satan will be released from his prison and will come out to deceive the nations that are at the four corners of the earth, Gog and Magog, to gather them for battle; their number is like the sand of the sea. And they marched up over the broad plain of the earth and surrounded the camp of the saints and the beloved city, but fire came down from heaven and consumed them, and the devil who had deceived them was thrown into the lake of fire and sulfur where the beast and the false prophet were, and they will be tormented day and night forever and ever.

So after Satan is defeated, he will be in a pit for a thousand years and unable to deceive man. But when he is released, he will be allowed to roam the earth trying to deceive nations into following him. He will attack God's people, but God will intervene and destroy his army, capture Satan, and cast him into the lake of fire forever.

You might ask why God would release Satan to go about deceiving the nations. The answer is that while Satan was in the pit, he could not deceive the people born during God's millennial reign. These people did not have a choice of who they would choose to be their king during this period. Satan was released to give those born during this utopian period the opportunity to choose whom they would prefer to be their King. God desires only those who choose Him to be their King to complete His ultimate plan.

Man was created for a purpose, but that purpose was not fulfilled once sin was defeated.

Psalm 147:4 reads,

> "He determines the number of the stars; he
> gives to all of them their names."

If God has called all the stars by name, is it not reasonable to believe that He has a purpose for them to fulfill? I believe His ultimate purpose is to use man, His physical creation, to rule as kings and priests not only on earth but over His physical population of all His chosen planets in the universe. Once Satan is finally defeated and cast into the lake of fire, God can proceed with His ultimate plan.

Spiritual rebirth was not available until God sent His Son

to die for the sins of mankind. The spiritually dead gain eternal life when they accept Jesus into their hearts. Until then, God provided a covering for man's sin; God gave animal skins to cover Adam's and Eve's nakedness and their sin. Life needed to be sacrificed to cover their sin. Death was the sentence for disobedience, but God would allow the death of a lamb as a substitute to cover man's sin until Jesus came as the perfect sacrifice that completely washed his sin away. Acceptance of Jesus into the heart is now the only way to resurrect a life that is spiritually dead and make it whole again providing everlasting life.

God is Spirit, and He created man with a spirit, a soul, and a body. The Bible reveals to us that God is Father, Son, and Holy Spirit, three in one. In understanding that man is body, spirit, and soul, we realize that we were created in God's image of three in one.

Other aspects of God's image are reflected in the fruits of the spirit recorded in Galatians 5:22–23.

> But the fruit of the Spirit is love, joy, peace, patience, kindness, goodness, faithfulness, gentleness, *self-control*; against such things there is no law. (Emphasis mine)

Jesus, when talking to Nicodemus in John 3:3–6, said,

> "Truly, truly, I say to you, unless one is *born again he cannot see the kingdom of God.*" Nicodemus said to him, "How can a man be born when he is old? Can he enter a second time into his mother's womb and be born?" Jesus answered, "Truly, truly, I say to you,

unless one is born of water and the Spirit, he cannot enter the kingdom of God. That which is born of the flesh is flesh, and that which is born of the Spirit is spirit." (Emphasis mine)

Jesus gives us an opportunity to become spiritually alive again by believing in Him as the Son of God who died for our sins, rose on the third day, and now sits at the right hand of the Father.

God is eternal; man was created by God to be eternal. Adam and Eve disobeyed God and spiritually died. Mankind, born physically alive, is still spiritually dead but eternal. Now, under the curse of the second death, dying physically while still spiritually dead means an eternity without God or living in His kingdom. Dying spiritually dead means existing eternally in a place prepared for the devil and his angels called the lake of fire.

God now affords us an opportunity to become spiritually alive again by believing in Jesus Christ as the Son of God, but it is our choice.

The Garden of Eden experience reveals to us that a problem we have all inherited in our spiritual realm causes us to react in the physical realm. Adam and Eve had to face the consequences of their choices, and we too will ultimately face the consequences of our choices and actions caused by this inner spiritual condition we call sin, a living, breathing entity residing in all of us. It must be dealt with or it will eventually destroy us.

Chapter 11

The Results of Lucifer's Decision

Revelation 13:8 (KJV) reads,

> "And all that dwell upon the earth shall worship him, [Satan] whose names are not written in the book of life of the Lamb slain from the foundation of the world."

Have you accepted Jesus as your Savior? This verse reveals a plan of redemption for us that was put in place before the foundation of the world. It also reveals that there are people who worship Satan, and their names are not included in God's Book of Life. Your body will die, but your spirit and soul will live forever. You will one day be resurrected to be judged. If you have not accepted God's provision for salvation, you will be sent to the eternal flames of the lake of fire. It is your choice.

Man was created to represent God on earth and rule over it. Genesis 1:28 tells us,

> And God blessed them. And God said to them, "be fruitful and multiply and fill the earth and subdue it, *and have dominion* over the fish of the sea and over the birds of the heavens and over every living thing that moves on the earth." (Emphasis mine)

Man was created to live forever physically as well as spiritually; he was to eat of the tree of life, but after Satan tricked Adam and Eve, they no longer had access to the fruit of the tree of life, and Satan stole their right to rule the earth.

When Satan tempted Jesus on the mount, he claimed ownership of earth.

> And the devil took him up and showed him all the kingdoms of the world in a moment of time, and said to him, "To you I will give all this authority and their glory, for it has been delivered to me, and I give it to whom I will." (Luke 4:5–6)

Adam and Eve's sin gave Satan the right to rule the earth; they sold their birthright for the fruit of the tree of the knowledge of good and evil.

When Satan usurped man's dominion over earth, God cast Adam and Eve out of the garden to fend for themselves as seen in Genesis 3:22–24.

> Then the LORD God said, 'Behold, the man has become like one of us in knowing good and evil. *Now, lest he reach out his hand and take also of the tree of life and eat, and live forever—* therefore the LORD God sent him out from the Garden of Eden to work the ground from which he was taken. He drove out the man, and at the east of the Garden of Eden he placed the cherubim and a flaming sword that turned every way to guard the way to the tree of life. (Emphasis mine)

Cast out of the garden, they no longer enjoyed its

comforts and would thus have to create their own comfort zone from what their new residence provided.

Disobedience brought death. They were spiritually dead but physically alive and had an appointment with death. Hebrews 9:27 reads,

> "And just as it is appointed for man to die once, and after that comes judgment."

Chapter 12

God's Plan for Mankind's Redemption

About two thousand years ago, God sent His Son into the world to be the sacrifice required for our sins. Jesus was born of the Virgin Mary but had no earthly father, so He was born without sin and lived a sin-free life for the purpose of being the sacrifice that would cover all our sins.

Jesus was physical just like you and me, and being physical, He had to die. He chose to die to be the sacrifice for our sin.

Hebrews 1:1–2 reads,

> Long ago, at many times and in many ways, God spoke to our fathers by the prophets, but in these last days he has spoken to us by his Son, whom he appointed the heir of all things, through whom also he created the world.

Christ, God in the flesh, was a physical being who was crucified and died. However, He was a victor over death; He was physically resurrected and is spiritually and physically alive in heaven. At their resurrection, believers will be like Him, both spiritually and physically alive.

In 1 John 3:2, we read,

> "Beloved, we are God's children now, and what we will be has not yet appeared; but we know that when he appears *we shall be like him,* because we shall see him as he is" (Emphasis mine).

What happens when man dies is mentioned in Hebrews 9:27

> And just as it is appointed for man to die once, and after that comes judgment,

In Genesis 3:19, God declared to Adam after his disobedience,

> "By the sweat of your face you shall eat bread, till you return to the ground, for out of it you were taken; for you are dust, and *to dust you shall return*" (Emphasis mine).

So the physical body returns to dust, but what about the spirit and soul? Ecclesiastes 12:7 (KJV) tells us,

> "Then shall the dust return to the earth as it was: and the spirit shall return unto God who gave it."

Ezekiel 18:20 (KJV) tells us,

> "The soul who sins shall die."

To understand what happens at death, we must look at the parable of the rich man and Lazarus as recorded in Luke 16:19–31 (KJV).

> There was a certain rich man, which was clothed in purple and fine linen, and fared sumptuously every day: And there was a certain beggar named Lazarus, which was laid at his gate, full of sores, And desiring to be fed with the crumbs which fell from the rich man's table: moreover the dogs came and licked his

sores.

And it came to pass, that the beggar died, and was carried by the angels into Abraham's bosom: the rich man also died, and was buried; And *in hell he lift up his eyes*, being in torments, and seeth Abraham afar off, and Lazarus in his bosom. And he cried and said, Father Abraham, have mercy on me, and send Lazarus, which he may dip the tip of his finger in water, and cool my tongue; for I am tormented in this flame.

But Abraham said, Son, remember that thou in thy lifetime receivedst thy good things, and likewise Lazarus evil things: but now he is comforted, and thou art tormented. And beside all this, between us and you there is a great gulf fixed: so that they which would pass from hence to you cannot; neither can they pass to us, which would come from thence. Then he said, I pray thee therefore, father, that thou wouldest send him to my father's house: For I have five brethren; that he may testify unto them, lest they also come into this place of torment. Abraham saith unto him, They have Moses and the prophets; let them hear them. And he said, Nay, father Abraham: but if one went unto them from the dead, they will repent. And he said unto him, If they hear not Moses and the prophets, neither will they be persuaded, though one rose from the dead. (Emphasis mine)

The rich man's soul went to hell and with it his senses

and communicative skills. There is nothing mentioned about his spirit as scripture has told us that "the Spirit returns to the God who gave it." Sinners have no ability to communicate with God following their deaths because all communication with God requires a spirit, and their spirits will have returned to God.

Even though the body dies and returns to dust, it will be resurrected for judgment and rejoined with the soul and go to heaven or be cast into the lake of fire.

It is your choice. You are God's property, and He sets the rules; any disobedience is sin and punishable by death. However, God put in place a plan of redemption for man if he chooses it and its conditions. The death the scriptures mention is not physical death but the death of the soul. The soul and the spirit will exist eternally. The death of the soul scripture tells us about is the second death mentioned in Revelation 21:8:

> "But as for the cowardly, the faithless, the detestable, as for murderers, the sexually immoral, sorcerers, idolaters, and all liars, *their portion will be in the lake that burns with fire and sulfur, which is the second death*" (Emphasis mine).

The second death occurs when the soul is cast into the lake of fire following the resurrection of the sinner's body and soul, which will be cast into the lake of fire.

Revelation 20:11–15 reads,

> Then I saw a great white throne and him who was seated on it. From his presence earth and

sky fled away, and no place was found for them. And I saw the dead, great and small, standing before the throne, and books were opened. Then another book was opened, which is the book of life. And the dead were judged by what was written in the books, according to what they had done. And the sea gave up the dead who were in it, Death and Hades gave up the dead who were in them, and they were judged, each one of them, according to what they had done. Then Death and Hades were thrown into the lake of fire. This is the second death, the lake of fire. And if anyone's name was not found written in the book of life, he was thrown into the lake of fire.

There is only one way to have your name recorded in the Book of Life—you must choose to accept Christ Jesus into your heart as your Redeemer.

When Christians die, their souls and spirits go to heaven, and they will be reunited by their bodies at the resurrection, and they will never die. Mark 12:25 reads,

> "For when they rise from the dead, they neither marry nor are given in marriage, *but are like angels in heaven*" (Emphasis mine).

So, at death, the body returns to dust, the spirit returns to God, and the soul goes to heaven or hell to await the final judgment depending on its relationship with God.

The spirit is necessary for us to have a relationship with God as John 4:24 says:

"God is spirit, and those who worship him must worship in spirit and truth."

The soul houses our intelligence and senses and our ability to make choices.

John 3:14–21 lays out God's plan for our redemption.

And as Moses lifted up the serpent in the wilderness, so must the Son of Man be lifted up, that whoever believes in him may have eternal life. For God so loved the world, that he gave his only Son, that whoever believes in him should not perish but have eternal life. For God did not send his Son into the world to condemn the world, but in order that the world might be saved through him. Whoever believes in him is not condemned, but whoever does not believe is condemned already, because he has not believed in the name of the only Son of God. And this is the judgment: the light has come into the world, and people loved the darkness rather than the light because their works were evil. For everyone who does wicked things hates the light and does not come to the light, lest his works should be exposed. But whoever does what is true comes to the light, so that it may be clearly seen that his works have been carried out in God.

So, "*Whoever believes in him* should not perish but have eternal life" (Emphasis mine). This is the belief we must accept in our hearts.

Chapter 13

The Comfort Zone

God had provided Adam and Eve all that they needed in their comfort zone, the Garden of Eden, which had boundaries. As I have mentioned, this comfort zone was their hearts, their boxes so to speak. We will now see what God said about this box.

In his efforts to defeat God, Satan intervened in God's plan for man by inserting his mentor into his heart, the area in which man makes decisions, the place where man has enthroned himself as king, not really understanding that the decisions he makes are really influenced by the helper or mentor he has allowed in as keeper of his box. God had placed within man His Holy Spirit to help him make good decisions. When Adam and Eve were enticed by Satan to disobey God, they allowed Satan to place his demonic influence into their boxes, replacing the Holy Spirit.

Eve was attacked in the physical realm; Satan played upon her physical desires—the beautiful tree and its fruit, which looked delicious. He wanted her physical desires to overcome her spiritual desires. The serpent told her she would "be like God, knowing good and evil" if she ate the fruit. He knew that if he could convince her that God had not been truthful about the fruit and that she would not really die but become a god, he would be able to replace the Holy Spirit in her heart with himself. In this way, he successfully inserted into mankind's heart hatred, jealousy, rage, murder, and other evil elements.

We immediately see the effects of Satan's plan of inserting his demonic influence into man, where the gifts of the Holy Spirit were present before Satan intervened. Now it was evident that this demonic influence was in charge as we see in the very next story in God's word.

Cain, the firstborn of Adam and Eve, killed Abel, as recorded in Genesis 4:3–8.

> In the course of time Cain brought to the LORD an offering of the fruit of the ground, and Abel also brought of the firstborn of his flock and of their fat portions. And the LORD had regard for Abel and his offering, but for Cain and his offering he had no regard. So, Cain was very angry, and his face fell.

> The LORD said to Cain, "Why are you angry, and why has your face fallen? If you do well, will you not be accepted? And if you do not do well, sin is crouching at the door. Its desire is for you, but you must rule over it." Cain spoke to Abel his brother. And when they were in the field, Cain rose up against his brother Abel and killed him.

Genesis 3:22 reads,

> "Then the LORD God said, 'Behold, the man has become like one of us in knowing good and evil. Now, lest he reach out his hand and take also of the tree of life and eat, and live forever.'" Adam and Eve had made the wrong choice.

Our power to choose resides in our comfort zone, where the soul is responsible for our decisions. The Bible refers to this as the heart. It's where God's Holy Spirit once resided to help us make the right decisions until Satan usurped the Holy Spirit's position there.

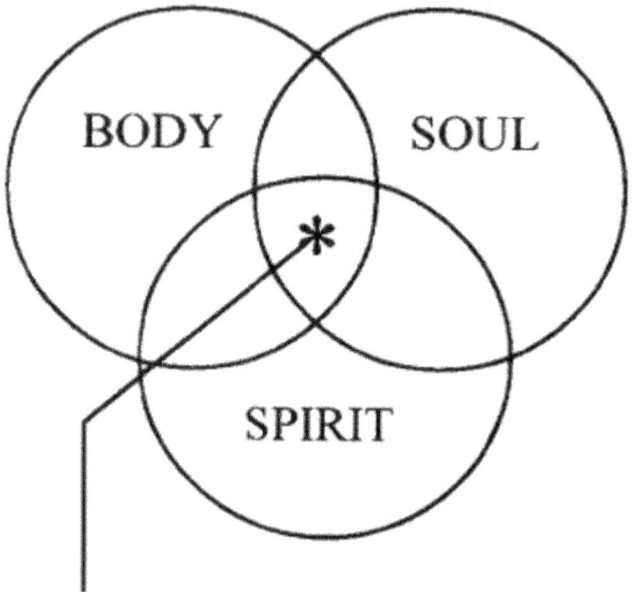

It is this area of our being where our decisions are made.

Our physical selves seem to carry much more weight than our spiritual selves. The physical is where we can see, hear, and touch things while the spiritual is residing in the background. We tend to not listen to the Spirit; we tend to give in to the physical desires of the flesh as Eve did; she gave to Adam and he ate.

Adam was not innocent in this episode; 1 Timothy 2:13–14 tells us that Eve was deceived but that Adam knew full well what he was doing. It was Adam's sin that caused all mankind to be born spiritually dead:

"For Adam was formed first, then Eve; and Adam was not deceived, but the woman was deceived and became a transgressor."

What really happened in the garden? Satan, probably speaking through the Serpent over a short period of time began to communicate with Eve. He eventually gained her confidence when he sprung upon her his real plan to deceive her and cause her to question God, claiming His ultimate motive was to keep her from being a god. If he was successful, he would subject Adam and Eve to his leadership and replace the Holy Spirit with his mentor.

Satan, however, was not omnipresent; he could indwell only one person at a time. This being the case, Satan appoints demonic influences to represent him as guides and mentors.

With the Holy Spirit no longer available to guide them, Adam and Eve died spiritually and lost eternal life; we have inherited from them that situation. We must be born again if we want to obtain life eternal.

Being spiritually dead means we must create our own comfort zones, for it is through them that we can rule our lives by setting boundaries and controlling our decisions and actions, all duties of our soul. We get help developing our comfort zones through our parents, friends, and relatives, but Satan wants in as well to deceive us. God desires to be involved, but His influence comes from outside our comfort zones if we have not accepted Christ as our Savior.

Now, man had a problem—how to carry out the tasks he was created to do. He no longer had the Holy Spirit to help guide and direct his decisions because Satan had taken His place in his heart. He could remain under the power of Satan or rebel against him and choose to return to God. That, however, would not be easy, as Satan would do all in his power to maintain his control of everyone attempting to return to God. But man still had the power of choice, and he could determine how to use that gift.

Parents restrict their children for their safety, but as the children grow, the parents lift restrictions one at a time as the children's growing maturity warrants. This allows children to create their own comfort zones and expand them as they grow up, all the while setting boundaries for themselves. They learn there are people, places, and activities that are not beneficial to their well-being.

Parents play an important role here; they are responsible for teaching their children that choices have consequences and that bad choices have bad consequences. It is the parents' responsibility to hold their children accountable for their bad choices and applaud them for their good choices. Parents do their children no favors if they are permissive and do not punish them for their wrongdoings and thus teach them the consequences. If children learn that their misbehavior does not result in punishment, that will teach them that their very bad behavior also has no meaningful consequences.

Proverbs 22:6 tells us,

> "Train up a child in the way he should go;
> even when he is old he will not depart from it."

The Catholics have a philosophy that basically says, "Give us a child until he is seven and he is mine for life."

Children learn right from wrong by watching and listening to their parents. They learn to love and have compassion or to be hateful and resentful. They will learn the good, the bad, and the ugly from their parents.

We all have to set up boundaries if they were not instilled in us. These boundaries are spiritual barriers warning us of the dangers lying outside our comfort zones. There are also character and ethical boundaries that need to be set inside our comfort zones. The Holy Spirit residing in our comfort zones will raise red flags or warnings when undesirable elements want in. Without the Holy Spirit's presence, Satan's demonic influence will welcome in such undesirable elements, the fruits of his demonic spirit.

Galatians 5:16–25 says,

> But I say, walk by the Spirit, and you will not gratify the desires of the flesh. For the desires of the flesh are against the Spirit, and the desires of the Spirit are against the flesh, for these are opposed to each other, to keep you from doing the things you want to do. But if you are led by the Spirit, you are not under the law. Now the works of the flesh are evident: sexual immorality, impurity, sensuality, idolatry, sorcery, enmity, strife, jealousy, fits of anger, rivalries, dissensions, divisions, envy, drunkenness, orgies, and things like these. I warn you, as I warned you before, that those who do such things will not inherit the kingdom of God. But the fruit of the Spirit is love, joy, peace, patience, kindness, goodness, faithfulness, gentleness, self-control; against such things there is no law. And those who belong to Christ Jesus have crucified the flesh with its passions and desires.

If we live by the Spirit, let us also keep in step with the Spirit.

Our physical selves are deeply aware of the physical realm in which we live but seem oblivious to the spiritual realm. The spirit in us will represents God's desire for our lives. He wants to communicate to us what those plans are for our lives, but we seem to ignore them. The soul, where we make decisions, seems to listen to fleshly desires and to our mentor (Satan or the Holy Spirit) to tell us what to do. The demonic influence will lead us to death while the Holy Spirit will lead us to everlasting life. Who is your mentor?

Chapter 14

Who Rules Your Box?

You probably have some good things and some bad things in your comfort zone, things that can allow you to do great things, and things that will urge you to do bad things. It is important for you to know what is inside your box because whatever is there is the controlling mechanism of your life.

One of the most powerful possessions you have in your box is your power to choose what resides in it and what you expel from it. The penalties for your bad choices may still have to be dealt with, but you can choose to eject any bad residents in your comfort zone.

Our bodies, souls, and spirits, which make up our boxes, can be assisted by the Holy Spirit to help guide us. These four work together like a committee to decide what actions to take, but the soul makes the final choice. Outside influences affect our decisions, and some come from the physical realm—family, friends, and others—while others come from Satan's spiritual realm.

Satan usurped man's God-given rights to rule the earth, and the Holy Spirit was cast out of the comfort zone and replaced by a demonic spirit appointed by Satan. This change now requires the Holy Spirit to influence us from outside our boxes unless we have accepted Jesus into our hearts as our Savior. Accepting Jesus in this way will cast Satan's demonic spirit out and be replaced by the Holy Spirit as our guide and counselor.

John 14:15–17 reads,

> If you love me, you will keep my commandments. And I will ask the Father, and he will give you *another Helper*, to be with you forever, even the Spirit of truth, whom the world cannot receive, because it neither sees him nor knows him. You know him, for *he dwells with you and will be in you.* (Emphasis mine)

The helper Jesus was telling His disciples about just before His crucifixion comforted them. This comforter was none other than the Holy Spirit.

If you were asked, "Who rules your box?" you would probably say, "I do," but do you? Have you always made right decisions? Where did those decisions come from? They did not come from your brain as you might believe; they came from your box, where your mentor resides. Your mentor does not always get his way, but his influence is a powerful force in your life. Your box has at least four inhabitants wrestling with the decisions you make—your flesh, your spirit, your soul, and your mentor. There may be a myriad of outside forces trying to influence your decisions, but in reality, it is these four elements (and particularly your body) that will rule your final decision. It is your soul that is responsible for the decisions you make, and that is where the buck stops.

Demonic spirits have always caused a great deal of trouble for those who housed them. Jesus often cast demons out of individuals, sometimes many demons out of the same person.

Mark 9:16–29 reads,

> And he asked them, "What are you arguing about with them?" And someone from the

crowd answered him, "Teacher, I brought my son to you, for he has a spirit that makes him mute. And whenever it seizes him, it throws him down, and he foams and grinds his teeth and becomes rigid. So I asked your disciples to cast it out, and they were not able."

And he answered them, "O faithless generation, how long am I to be with you? How long am I to bear with you? Bring him to me." And they brought the boy to him. And when the spirit saw him, immediately it convulsed the boy, and he fell on the ground and rolled about, foaming at the mouth.

And Jesus asked his father, "How long has this been happening to him?" And he said, "From childhood. And it has often cast him into fire and into water, to destroy him. But if you can do anything, have compassion on us and help us." And Jesus said to him, "'If you can'! All things are possible for one who believes."

Immediately the father of the child cried out and said, "I believe; help my unbelief!" And when Jesus saw that a crowd came running together, he rebuked the unclean spirit, saying to it, "*You mute and deaf spirit, I command you, come out of him and never enter him again.*" And after crying out and convulsing him terribly, it came out, and the boy was like a corpse, so that most of them said, "He is dead." But Jesus took him by the hand and lifted him up, and he arose.

And when he had entered the house, his

disciples asked him privately, "Why could we not cast it out?" And he said to them, "This kind cannot be driven out by anything but prayer." (Emphasis mine)

Matthew 9:32–34 tells us,

As they were going away, behold, a demon-oppressed man who was mute was brought to him.

And when the demon had been cast out, the mute man spoke. And the crowds marveled, saying, "Never was anything like this seen in Israel."

But the Pharisees said, "He casts out demons by the prince of demons." (Emphasis mine)

Luke 8:1–2 reads,

Soon afterward he went on through cities and villages, proclaiming and bringing the good news of the kingdom of God. And the twelve were with him, and also some women who had been healed of evil spirits and infirmities: Mary, called Magdalene, from whom seven demons had gone out.

Matthew 12:22 reads,

"Then a demon-oppressed man who was blind and mute was brought to him, and he healed him, so that the man spoke and saw."

See also Matthew 8:28–35 and Mark 5:9–20, where Jesus cast a legion of demons out of one person.

These demons reside in your box, and they will try to influence your decisions. Demonic possession was a common occurrence in Jesus's day, and it is no different today. Why are there so many evil fruits such as murder, stealing, lying, cheating, envy, hatred, and so many others prevalent in society? These are all fruits of a demonic influence residing in a nonbeliever's box that you may not even realize he is there.

"The devil made me do it" is more of a reality than we may realize. If God's Holy Spirit is not residing in your box, there's a hundred percent chance that a demonic spirit is dwelling there and maybe more than one.

When we accept Jesus as our Savior into our hearts, the Holy Spirit takes up residence there. The demonic spirit will be expelled, but it will remain an influence working from outside our box. He will attack our weaknesses by temptation just as he attacked Eve in the garden from outside her heart.

The Holy Spirit will begin to cleanse your comfort zone by changing it from the inside out. It will take time, and He will need cooperation from the other occupants of your comfort zone, namely, your body, soul, and spirit. If you allow the Holy Spirit to work, He will begin to change your fruit from evil to good.

Our infirmities are most likely a medical condition. However, I would not rule out the demonic, but it seems to be rare.

John 14:15–31 tells us,

> "If you love me, you will keep my commandments. And I will ask the Father, and he will give you another Helper, to be with you forever, even the Spirit of truth, whom the world cannot receive, because it neither sees him nor knows him. You know him, for he dwells with you and *will be in you.* I will not leave you as orphans; I will come to you. Yet a little while and the world will see me no more, but you will see me. Because I live, you also will live. In that day you will know that I am in my Father, and you in me, and I in you. Whoever has my commandments and keeps them, he it is who loves me. And he who loves me will be loved by my Father, and I will love him and manifest myself to him."

> Judas (not Iscariot) said to him, "Lord, how is it that you will manifest yourself to us, and not to the world?" Jesus answered him, "If anyone loves me, he will keep my word, and my Father will love him, and we will come to him and make our home with him. Whoever does not love me does not keep my words. And the word that you hear is not mine but the Father's who sent me. These things I have spoken to you while I am still with you. But the Helper, the Holy Spirit, whom the Father will send in my name, he will teach you all things and bring to your remembrance all that I have said to you. Peace I leave with you; my peace I give to you.

Not as the world gives do I give to you. Let not your hearts be troubled, neither let them be afraid. You heard me say to you, 'I am going away, and I will come to you.' If you loved me, you would have rejoiced, because I am going to the Father, for the Father is greater than I.

"And now I have told you before it takes place, so that when it does take place you may believe. I will no longer talk much with you, for the ruler of this world is coming. He has no claim on me, but I do as the Father has commanded me, so that the world may know that I love the Father. Rise, let us go from here." (Emphasis mine)

If you are not a believer in Jesus Christ, you have this demonic spirit residing in your box. It causes people to do all sorts of evil and could be responsible for some of their infirmities. This demonic spirit may also invite other demonic spirits into your box. You may be able to sometimes suppress his activities, but eventually, his demonic influence will reveal itself.

In Luke 11:24–26, Jesus told us what happened when a spirit was cleaned out of an individual.

When the unclean spirit has gone out of a person, it passes through waterless places seeking rest, and finding none it says, "I will return to my house from which I came." And when it comes, it finds the house swept and put in order. Then it goes and brings seven other spirits more evil than itself, and they enter and dwell there. And the last state of that person is worse than the first.

You may be able to rid a demonic spirit through exorcisms, but if your box does not contain the Holy Spirit, which requires a belief in Jesus as the Son of God, you are susceptible to more demonic spirits invading your cleaned-up box.

Chapter 15

The Box—Heart or Comfort Zone

In 1981, my father was on his deathbed. He had suffered a stroke that had affected his speech to the point that he could not put his words together so that they were understandable, which frustrated him tremendously. A day or two before his death, I was alone with him when he, with much difficulty asked me to pray with him.

Then something happened that I cannot explain as anything other than an act of God. I asked my father to pray, knowing full well the problem he had communicating. So why did I even ask him to pray unless it was God ordained? What happened next was a confirmation that God was in control of the whole situation. My father agreed and prayed with a completely understandable prayer—not a word out of place. My faith was magnified greatly; I believed I had witnessed a miracle.

Immediately after the prayer, he again was unable to communicate properly. So what really happened there? Was it really a miracle? Or did he enter a spiritual realm that was unaffected by his stroke? I knew, however, that God had given me a gift I needed—knowing that He was in the room with my father in his time of need.

Matthew 6:5–6 (KJV) reveals to us what Jesus says about prayer.

> And when thou prayest, thou shalt not be
> as the hypocrites are: for they love to pray
> standing in the synagogues and in the corners

of the streets, that they may be seen of men. Verily I say unto you, They have their reward. But thou, when thou prayest, *enter into thy closet*, and when thou hast *shut thy door*, pray to thy Father which is in secret; and thy Father which seeth in secret shall reward thee openly. (Emphasis mine)

I believe that when Jesus told us to enter our closet, He was referring to what I call our boxes, the areas where the soul, body, and spirit are in control of our decision making. It is there He wants us to commune with Him. By shutting the door, He wants us to close out all distractions and focus a hundred percent on our relationship with Him.

Chapter 16

Abraham

The story of God's dealing with man is found in the history of His establishing the Israelites as His people. All their successes and failures are shown to us in their story. Their story is a corporate dealing with a nation that represents how God now deals with us as individuals.

God's Calling

Abram was living in a place called Ur of the Chaldees, a city fraught with idolatrous worship when God began to deal with him about leaving that place and going to a place where God could begin to change him.

Genesis 12:1 reads,

> "Now the LORD said to Abram, 'Go from your country and your kindred and your father's house to the land that I will show you.'"

What God was really saying to Abram was, "Get out of your comfort zone." Just how God communicated that to Abram we do not know; it could have been an audible voice or an inner voice, a feeling that he needed to leave. Regardless, he felt his circumstances would not or could not change unless he left Ur based on God's urging.

Genesis 12:1–3 reads,

> Now the LORD said to Abram, "Go from your country and your kindred and your father's house to the land that I will show you. And I will make of you a great nation, and I will bless you and make your name great, so that you will be a blessing. I will bless those who bless you, and him who dishonors you I will curse, and in you all the families of the earth shall be blessed."

Abram was seventy-five when he left Haran following his father's death, but he had no children. Sarai, his wife, was barren. Abram, however, believed God when He promised Abram in Genesis 12:7:

> "Then the LORD appeared to Abram and said, *'To your offspring I will give this land.'* So he built there an altar to the LORD, who had appeared to him" (Emphasis mine).

Abraham's faith was strong enough to believe even in his old age that God would fulfill His promise.

In the years between God's promise and the birth of Isaac, fulfilling God's promise, many events in Abram's life occurred.

- They journeyed to Egypt because of a famine. (Genesis 12:10)
- There was a conflict with Pharaoh. (Genesis 12:11–20)
- Abram and his nephew Lot separated. (Genesis 13:1–

12)

- Abram rescued Lot following a war. (Genesis 14:1–16)
- Abram encountered Melchizedek, priest of the highest God. (Genesis 14:17–24)
- Sarai gave her servant Hagar to Abram to birth a child for her. A conflict occurred between Sarai and Hagar. (Genesis 16:1–16)
- The covenant of circumcision instituted. Abram's name changed to Abraham. (Genesis 17:1–14)
- Sarai gave birth to Isaac in her old age, and God changed her name to Sarah. (Genesis 17:15–21)

Abraham was a hundred and Sarah was ninety when their son, Isaac, was born.

God tested Abraham in Genesis 22:1–2 and 9–13.

> After these things God tested Abraham and said to him, "Abraham!" And he said, "Here I am." He said, "Take your son, your only son Isaac, whom you love, and go to the land of Moriah, and offer him there as a burnt offering on one of the mountains of which I shall tell you."

> When they came to the place of which God had told him, Abraham built the altar there and laid the wood in order and bound Isaac his son and laid him on the altar, on top of the wood. Then Abraham reached out his hand and took the knife to slaughter his son. But the angel of the LORD called to him from heaven and said, "Abraham, Abraham!" And he said, "Here I am."

He said, "Do not lay your hand on the boy or do anything to him, for now I know that you fear God, seeing you have not withheld your son, your only son, from me."

And Abraham lifted up his eyes and looked, and behold, behind him was a ram, caught in a thicket by his horns. And Abraham went and took the ram and offered it up as a burnt offering instead of his son.

Chapter 17

Isaac and Jacob

Isaac was 37 when his mother died at age 127. Abraham sent his servant, Eliezer, to his relatives in Haran to get a wife for Isaac, and he brought back Rebekah, the granddaughter of Nahor, Abraham's brother.

Isaac had two sons through Rebekah, Esau and Jacob, twins, of which Jacob was the second one born. It was through Jacob that twelve sons were born who became the twelve tribes or patriarchs of the Israelites. God changed Jacob's name to Israel (see Genesis 32:28). Of the twelve sons born to Jacob, Joseph was the eleventh, the first-born child of his wife Rachel.

Here is what Genesis 37:3–11 tells us about Joseph.

Now Israel loved Joseph more than any other of his sons, because he was the son of his old age. And he made him a robe of many colors. But when his brothers saw that their father loved him more than all his brothers, they hated him and could not speak peacefully to him. Now Joseph had a dream, and when he told it to his brothers they hated him even more. He said to them, "Hear this dream that I have dreamed: Behold, we were binding sheaves in the field, and behold, my sheaf arose and stood upright. And behold, your sheaves gathered around it and bowed down to my sheaf." His brothers said to him, "Are you indeed to reign over us? Or are you indeed to rule over us?" So they hated him even more for his dreams and for his words. Then he dreamed another dream and told it to his brothers and said, "Behold, I have dreamed another dream. Behold, the sun, the moon, and eleven stars were bowing down to me." But when he told it to his father and to his brothers, his father rebuked him and said to him, "What is this dream that you have dreamed? Shall I and your mother and your brothers indeed come to bow ourselves to the ground before you?" And his brothers were jealous of him, but his father kept the saying in mind.

Joseph's brothers were tending their flocks when his father told him to go and check on his brothers. When they saw Joseph coming, they plotted to kill him, but they ended up selling him to a caravan of traders who eventually sold him as a slave to an Egyptian named Potiphar (see Genesis 37:18–36).

Though he was a slave, Joseph maintained his integrity and ethics, which caused him to be cast into prison. While in prison, he was exalted to maintain order. Two of the inmates had had dreams that Joseph interpreted for them. These two dream interpretations proved to be true when one lost his life and the other returned to his former position as cupbearer to Pharaoh.

Eventually, Pharaoh had a dream that bothered him, but he did not understand it. He sought the magicians to interpret his dreams, but they could not. The cupbearer told Pharaoh that Joseph had interpreted his dream, so Pharaoh summoned Joseph and told him about his dream. Joseph told Pharaoh that there would be seven years of plenty in their crops followed by seven years of famine. This information resulted in Pharaoh making Joseph second in line to himself. He was put in charge of all of Egypt's crops and storing them for use during the famine years. God orchestrated all these events to bring Joseph from Canaan to Egypt.

This famine involved Egypt and the surrounding areas including Canaan, where Jacob and his family lived. Jacob heard about the food supply in Egypt and sent ten of his eleven sons to Egypt to buy food. Benjamin, Joseph's younger brother, was left in Canaan. The brothers arrived in Egypt not knowing that they would be dealing with their brother they had sold as a slave. Joseph questioned his brothers, who did not recognize him. He sought information about his family, but he did not reveal to them who he was. Long story short, Joseph eventually revealed who he was and proclaimed that it was God who had sent him to Egypt.

God's plan was to get Jacob's family into Egypt, into the best part of the land to prepare them to be a nation. Jacob's obedience resulted in his family, seventy in number, going to Egypt because of the severe famine (Genesis 46:26–27).

They became a nation and lived in Egypt for some 430 years (Genesis 12: 40). They would eventually be enslaved by the Egyptians, who served many gods.

When Joseph entered Egypt, he gave them some instructions; Genesis 46:33–34.

> When Pharaoh calls you and says, "What is your occupation?" you shall say, "Your servants have been keepers of livestock from our youth even until now, both we and our fathers," in order that you may dwell in the land of Goshen,

> *for every shepherd is an abomination to the Egyptians.* (Emphasis mine)

In Genesis 47:2–3, we read,

> And from among his brothers he took five men and presented them to Pharaoh. Pharaoh said to his brothers, "What is your occupation?" And they said to Pharaoh, "Your servants are shepherds, as our fathers were."

This probably helped keep the Israelites from comingling with the Egyptians. It was under these circumstances that God prepared a leader named Moses who, under God's direction, would lead them out of Egyptian bondage. Egypt, a type of sin's bondage, refused to let the Israelites go into the wilderness to worship their God. God then instructed Moses to send plagues upon the Egyptians each one focusing on one of their gods. Pharaoh refused to let the Israelites depart until the tenth plague struck down all the Egyptians' firstborn. The Israelites there were protected from this plague by putting the blood of a lamb on their doorposts; the blood protected them from the death angel when he passed over to kill the firstborn of Egypt. This act was known as the Passover, which the Israelites were instructed to celebrate every year. Finally, Pharaoh relented and allowed the Israelites to depart, but then he changed his mind and pursued them with his army.

Fear came upon the people when they realized that Pharaoh and his army were approaching them. God placed a pillar of cloud between Pharaoh and his army and the Israelites to protect them. They ended up trapped between the Red Sea and Pharaoh's army, but God performed the greatest miracle of all by parting the Red Sea and thus permitting the Israelites to cross on dry ground into the desert. Pharaoh pursued them, and God allowed the Red Sea to return, which destroyed Pharaoh and his army.

It was in a wilderness desert area that God gave Moses the Ten Commandments and instructed him to build an ark to contain them. Moses was instructed to build a tabernacle and all the furnishings for it. This tabernacle would be enclosed by a fence-like structure made of fine twisted linen. Within this tabernacle would be a place called the holy of holies, where the Ark of the Covenant would be. This tabernacle would be the heart of their corporate society.

Chapter 18

The Pillar of Cloud and the Pillar of Fire

Exodus 13:21–22 tells us,

> And the LORD went before them by day in a pillar of cloud to lead them along the way, and by night in a pillar of fire to give them light, that they might travel by day and by night. The pillar of cloud by day and the pillar of fire by night *did not depart* from before the people. (Emphasis mine)

Whenever the pillar began to move away from the tabernacle, it was the Lord telling them to follow where He was leading them. They followed but were fearful and constantly complained about their food and water. So God provided manna, quail, and water throughout their forty-year wilderness journey.

God led them to the Promised Land after a two-year journey and told them to rid the land of all idolatrous worshippers, but they refused to enter because of fear of the giants living there. As a punishment for their disobedience, God allowed all over age twenty to die in the wilderness before they could make another attempt to enter.

Joshua and Caleb, who were two of the twelve sent into the Promised Land to spy out the land, were the only two who wanted to go in. They were the only ones above age twenty permitted to go into the Promised Land. (See Numbers 13:1–33 to read the account of the spies.)

Chapter 19

The Promised Land

After forty years of wandering in the wilderness, the Israelites were ready to move into the Promised Land, which had been promised to Abraham several hundred years earlier. Joshua would be their leader as Moses was not permitted to go in; he died in the wilderness. God gave instructions to them when they went into their new, God-given property.

It was a good land flowing with milk and honey, meaning that it was very productive land. It was however, filled with an idolatrous population. One in particular required human sacrifice. God gave the Israelites some instructions about this in Deuteronomy 7:1–2.

> When the LORD your God brings you into the land that you are entering to take possession of it, and clears away many nations before you, the Hittites, the Girgashites, the Amorites, the Canaanites, the Perizzites, the Hivites, and the Jebusites, seven nations more numerous and mightier than you, and when the LORD your God gives them over to you, and you defeat them, then you must devote them to complete destruction. You shall make no covenant with them and show no mercy to them.

God wanted the Israelites to destroy these idolatrous nations because He did not want them in the Israelites' comfort zone where they could be detrimental to their relationship with God.

Chapter 20

God Commissioned Joshua

Joshua 1:1–6 reads,

> After the death of Moses the servant of the LORD, the LORD said to Joshua the son of Nun, Moses' assistant, Moses my servant is dead. Now therefore arise, go over this Jordan, you and all this people, into the land that I am giving to them, to the people of Israel. Every place that the sole of your foot will tread upon I have given to you, just as I promised to Moses. From the wilderness and this Lebanon as far as the great river, the river Euphrates, all the land of the Hittites to the Great Sea toward the going down of the sun shall be your territory. No man shall be able to stand before you all the days of your life. Just as I was with Moses, so I will be with you. I will not leave you or forsake you. Be strong and courageous, for you shall cause this people to inherit the land that I swore to their fathers to give them.

Joshua followed God's instructions and won the battle of Jericho. The win, however, was short lived; when they went to fight Ai, a town smaller than Jericho, they were defeated because of their disobedience at the battle of Jericho.

The LORD said to Joshua, "Get up! Why have you fallen on your face? Israel has sinned; they have transgressed my covenant that I commanded them; they have taken some of the devoted things; they have stolen and lied and put them among their own belongings." (Joshua 7:10–11)

After a search for the guilty party, they found that Achan had taken things that were to be devoted to the Lord and hid them in his tent (see Joshua 7:10–26). God was dealing with a corporate people; when one sinned, they all sinned and were guilty.

God was with Joshua as he led Israel to defeat the nations, and the land was divided up between the tribes of Israel. However, they were never able to totally annihilate the seven nations that resided in their new comfort zone.

From the death of Joshua and through the many judges that God would appoint and the establishment of a king in Israel, the Israelites had an up-and-down relationship with God. The nations that were not annihilated caused Israel to accept many of their idol worship practices, a constant problem during the history of Israel in the Old Testament.

What does this biblical story dealing with corporate Israel show how God now deals with us as individuals?

- Sin will enslave you to do its bidding as Egypt enslaved Israel to do its bidding.
- When you call upon God, He will bring heaven and earth together on your behalf as He did for Israel in Egypt.
- Sin will do all in its power to fight back the forces of good as did Egypt in its attempt to keep Israel from leaving.

- Once you are delivered from sin, sin will pursue you as Egypt pursued Israel when it left.
- God will part the sea to deliver you from sin's grasp just as He delivered Israel from Egypt's grasp.
- God wants to lead you as He led the Israelites not by a pillar but through the guidance of the Holy Spirit.
- Once you are delivered (redeemed), God will begin to work in your heart to clean out the undesirable residents.
- As He gave Israel the laws He wanted them to live by, He will write His laws upon your heart and they will become a part of you.

The tabernacle, which held some manna and Aaron's rod as well as the Ten Commandments, represents our body as the temple that God declared was the temple of the Holy Spirit. The Ark of the Covenant was the heart of Israelite worship and is now our hearts wherein He writes His law. It was placed in a room of the tabernacle called the holy of holies, where God's presence resided. This tabernacle represents us when in the New Testament we are referred to as the temple of the Holy Spirit.

Jeremiah 31:33 tells us that a time would come when God would write His Commandments on our hearts, where our decisions are actually made and where our bodies, souls, spirits, and mentors reside. We know in our hearts what is right and wrong. If the Holy Spirit is residing in our hearts, we will act on what is right, but if Satan's demonic spirit is there, we will be subject to acting otherwise. When we accept Jesus into our hearts, He will through the Holy Spirit slowly begin to remove those detrimental elements residing in our hearts to bring forth the good fruit. *Galatians 5:16–26* tells us,

But I say, walk by the Spirit, and you will not gratify the desires of the flesh. For the desires of the flesh are against the Spirit, and the desires of the Spirit are against the flesh, for these are opposed to each other, to keep you from doing the things you want to do. But if you are led by the Spirit, you are not under the law. Now the works of the flesh are evident: sexual immorality, impurity, sensuality, idolatry, sorcery, enmity, strife, jealousy, fits of anger, rivalries, dissensions, divisions, envy, drunkenness, orgies, and things like these. I warn you, as I warned you before, that those who do such things will not inherit the kingdom of God.

But the fruit of the Spirit is love, joy, peace, patience, kindness, goodness, faithfulness, gentleness, self-control; against such things there is no law. And those who belong to Christ Jesus have crucified the flesh with its passions and desires. If we live by the Spirit, let us also keep in step with the Spirit. Let us not become conceited, provoking one another, envying one another.

Chapter 21

Job's Box

Job 1:1–12 tells us this.

There was a man in the land of Uz whose name was Job, and that man was blameless and upright, one who feared God and turned away from evil. There were born to him seven sons and three daughters. He possessed 7,000 sheep, 3,000 camels, 500 yoke of oxen, and 500 female donkeys, and very many servants, so that this man was the greatest of all the people of the east. His sons used to go and hold a feast in the house of each one on his day, and they would send and invite their three sisters to eat and drink with them.

And when the days of the feast had run their course, Job would send and consecrate them, and he would rise early in the morning and offer burnt offerings according to the number of them all. For Job said, "It may be that my children have sinned, and cursed God in their hearts." Thus Job did continually. Now there was a day when the sons of God came to present themselves before the LORD, and Satan also came among them. The LORD said to Satan, "From where have you come?" Satan answered the LORD and said, "From going to and fro on the earth, and from walking up and down on it."

And the LORD said to Satan, "Have you considered my servant Job, that there is none like him on the earth, a blameless and upright man, who fears God and turns away from evil?"

Then Satan answered the LORD and said, "Does Job fear God for no reason? Have you not put a hedge around him and his house and all that he has, on every side? You have blessed the work of his hands, and his possessions have increased in the land. But stretch out your hand and touch all that he has, and he will curse you to your face."

And the LORD said to Satan, "Behold, all that he has is in your hand. Only against him do not stretch out your hand. So, Satan went out from the presence of the LORD."

We have here a picture of a righteous man who managed his box correctly. Satan declared that God had a hedge, a box, around him so that nothing could penetrate it.

Satan wasn't wrong in his assumption that God was responsible for erecting a hedge, a comfort zone, around us. It is our conscience, which tells us something is not right. However, it wasn't God who maintained this restrictive force around Job; it was Job himself who was responsible for his hedge of protection just as Adam and Eve were responsible for the care of their garden, their box. Job wasn't about to let anything resembling sin or sinful activities into his box. This hedge was God's creation, but Job was responsible for its contents. All Job did or owned was in this box. He protected it with all that he had. Satan knew that the way Job was handling his box made it nearly impossible to penetrate.

When Job even thought that sin may be trying to invade his space, he took steps to eradicate it; for example, when his children feasted in their own homes, Job offered sacrifices just in case they had sinned. So Satan's assumption that the hedge was God's doing was only partially correct.

The protection afforded Job was the result of Job keeping his Box clean of any type of evil or sinful influences. Since Job would not allow these evil or sinful influences into his box, he was exempt from the price these influences would have otherwise cost him.

For example, when the Israelites came out of Egypt, God gave them a list of foods they were to consider clean to eat. If they ate only these clean foods, none of the diseases of Egypt would be upon them. They were protected by not eating unclean food or allowing it to be a part of their life.

It was right choices in every area of Job's life that maintained his impenetrable box. God was so confident of Job that He allowed Satan to attack Job's box. In the course of time, Job was attacked by Satan with the express purpose of getting Job to turn his back on God. Satan is doing everything in his power to attack God's people. When God allows Satan to attack us, it is with restrictions. If God allows Satan to attack a child of God, He blesses His child with overflowing benefits when the battle is over. He promises us to not allow anything to happen to us that we cannot handle.

In 1 Corinthians 10:13, we read,

No temptation has overtaken you that is not common to man. God is faithful, and he will not let you be tempted beyond your ability, *but with the temptation he will also provide the way of escape, that you may be able to endure it.* (Emphasis mine)

In one day, Job lost everything including his sons and daughters and all his livestock, yet he did not turn his back on God. Job knew in his heart that he had not sinned and refused to blame God for the bad things that had happened to him. Satan's tactics failed not because of what he had done to Job but because of how Job maintained his integrity and protected his box.

Satan again was given permission to attack Job's physical body but could not touch his life. The attack by Satan was with painful sores from his head to his feet (see Job 2:1–10).

His wife told him to "curse God and die," but again, Job knew his problems were not due to his sinning because he knew his life was pure before God. Job did not allow Satan to attack his box and convince him to turn his back on God; it was a battle for Job's soul. Job's friends told him that he must have sinned, but Job never gave in to their accusations as his heart felt no guilt because he was righteous before God. e. (Read Job 2:11 through to the end of the book.)

Satan was unable to penetrate Job's box; he accused God of constructing a hedge around Job to protect him. In reality, however, it was Job maintaining the hedge around him by not allowing evil or destructive thoughts to enter his mind no matter how deceptive those thoughts were.

It is also evident God must have been in Job's box directing his path. Satan realized he could not attack Job through his mind no matter how hard he tried.

Chapter 22

Saul

Saul was a learned man, a Pharisee who was very zealous concerning his faith. He knew Judaism frontward and backward. In his heart, he was a Jew's Jew knowing the law and blameless according to it. He was so zealous for Judaism that he desired greatly to quell the new sect called at the time the Way, Christianity, which in its very early years was growing exponentially and was of great concern to the priesthood of Judaism.

Paul was a determined individual with a great desire to do his part in putting down this new force that had sprung from the roots of Judaism. He considered it very detrimental and destructive. In his heart, he felt deeply that he was doing God's service. He tried to maintain his box and keep it clean according to the teaching that he had received from the renowned teacher of the law, Gamaliel (see Acts 22:3).

One day, he took an entourage of like-minded individuals to Damascus; he wanted to bring back in chains all he could find who had accepted Christ as their Savior. God on the other hand had a different plan for Saul's life.

Acts 9:4–6 tells us what happened to Saul on his way to Damascus.

> And he fell to the earth, and heard a voice saying unto him, Saul, Saul, why persecutest thou me? And he said, Who art thou, Lord? And the Lord said, I am Jesus whom thou persecutest: it is hard for thee to kick against the pricks. And he trembling and astonished said, Lord, what wilt thou have me to do?" And the Lord said unto him, Arise, and go into the

> city, and it shall be told thee what thou must
> do.

That encounter changed his life as he made a complete turnaround; he saw the light, you might say. God was rearranging his box and discarding the destructive associations, attitudes, and teaching he held so dearly. His life would never be the same as the hunter became the hunted. His old was discarded, and a new mission was given to him.

He suddenly realized that he was really working against God instead of for God. He repented of his ways and accepted a new way of life. He brought Jesus Christ into his heart, and Jesus Christ was in control of Saul rather than Saul being in control of himself. Actually, it was Satan who had had control of Saul. The change was so dramatic and complete that Saul's name was changed to Paul (see Acts 13:9).

Paul went on to take the gospel of Jesus Christ to the Gentiles—all who were not Jewish. He became the most prolific writer of the New Testament explaining God's plan of salvation to a lost and dying world.

The change in your life most likely will not be as dramatic as that of Saul's, but rest assured that when you accept Jesus Christ into your life, changes will be made as His plans will begin to be implemented. A rearrangement of your box will take place. This rearrangement will most likely be gradual as the Holy Spirit begins to rid your box of the bad fruit in your life and to replace it with good fruit (see Galatians 5:16–25).

You may not even realize that changes are occurring as they will be subtle. But rest assured changes will happen as

God, through the Holy Spirit does His work to help make you a better person.

Chapter 23

Get Out of the Box

God's Word has revealed to us the possibilities of what we can do when God directs us to get out of our boxes. He directed Noah to get out of his box and build an ark to save humanity from total destruction. Noah listened to God and did what He asked him to do.

He asked Moses to get out of his box and deliver God's people from their Egyptian bondage. Moses argued with God about that but finally relented when God would not take no for an answer. Moses became the greatest prophet in Israel because he got out of his box and did what God directed.

Noah and Moses are two extreme examples of what can be accomplished when we obey God's request to get out of our box. Getting out of the box can be a great blessing to us and to others if it is God who is asking us to do that. However, when we are asked by others, it can be devastating to us. How many lives have been destroyed by so-called friends asking people to get out of their boxes and try drugs or alcohol or engage in sinful activities? The problem of getting out of the box is bringing such things into your box.

Mark tells us that Jesus was confronted by the Pharisees about His disciples' eating without washing their hands.

> And the Pharisees and the scribes asked him, "Why do your disciples not walk according to the tradition of the elders, but eat with defiled hands?" (Mark 7:5)

Jesus chided them.

> And he called the people to him again and said to them, "Hear me, all of you, and understand: There is nothing outside a person that by going into him can defile him, but the things that come out of a person are what defile him." (Mark 7:14–15)

Later, when the disciples were gathered together, they asked Him about what He meant by His response to the Pharisees.

> And he said to them, "Then are you also without understanding? Do you not see that whatever goes into a person from outside cannot defile him, since it enters not his heart but his stomach, and is expelled?" (Thus he declared all foods clean.) And he said, "What comes out of a person is what defiles him. For from within, out of the heart of man, come evil thoughts, sexual immorality, theft, murder, adultery, coveting, wickedness, deceit, sensuality, envy, slander, pride, foolishness. All these evil things come from within, and they defile a person." (Mark 18:23)

So getting out of the box is not the problem; it is what is in the box that will reveal itself. The only effective way to fix your box is to invite Jesus into your heart; He will bring with Him the Holy Spirit to help cleanse your box of evil and bring in the good.

Chapter 24

What Have We Learned?

We have learned from the story of Adam and Eve that God created us with bodies to carry out our duties of taking care of planet Earth. God planted within us souls with the intelligence to accomplish the task. He also placed within us a spirit for the purpose of communicating with Him and to give life to the flesh.

We also see that we were created in the image of God. We found that God's Holy Spirit was dwelling in man before he fell. We learned also that with the Holy Spirit came the gifts of "joy, peace, patience, kindness, goodness, faithfulness, gentleness, self-control; against such things there is no law" (Galatian 5:22–23).

We have discovered that man was designed to live forever. But when he disobeyed God's commands he lost everlasting life as they were cast out of the garden to prevent them from eating from the tree of life. They also lost the Holy Spirit, which was replaced by a demonic spirit that brought with him "sexual immorality, impurity, sensuality, idolatry, sorcery, enmity, strife, jealousy, fits of anger, rivalries, dissensions, divisions, envy, drunkenness, orgies, and things like these. I warn you, as I warned you before, that those who do such things will not inherit the kingdom of God" (Galatians 5:19–21).

We have discovered in the book of Job that Satan is not our friend, which he is out to destroy those who have accepted God's way. His goal is for us to turn from God and to him. Satan is so devious that he will do anything in his power to destroy us. We have also learned that God will use

Satan's devious plans to destroy to ultimately bless those who have remained faithful to Him.

We have learned that mankind is God's property and that He designed us for a purpose. Even though we have been born with a desire to sin, God wants us back.

John 3:16–18 reads,

> For God so loved the world, that he gave his only Son, that whoever believes in him should not perish but have eternal life. For God did not send his Son into the world to condemn the world, but in order that the world might be saved through him. Whoever believes in him is not condemned, but whoever does not believe is condemned already, because he has not believed in the name of the only Son of God.

God loved His creation so much that He sent His only Son to pay the price for mankind's redemption. He wants you back. He has a plan for your life, but that plan can be accomplished only if you invite Him into your heart. That plan is encoded in your DNA and will be worked out with the advice of the Holy Spirit residing in your heart. You still have your free will at work; it will still be your choice to accept or reject His advice.

Satan is determined to use his power to convince you that you don't need to accept God's provision, he says, "All you have to do to go to heaven is to do good works to outweigh your bad works." That is another lie conceived by Satan to keep you in his fold.

God's Word declares that all you need to do is accept

Jesus into your heart as His Son, who sacrificed His life to pay the ransom required for your sins. Once you are forgiven, good works will follow. Good works however can never pay the price required as a ransom for your soul. Jesus paid the ransom. Accepting Jesus for who He is the only requirement.

Acts 16:25–31 tells us this.

> About midnight Paul and Silas were praying and singing hymns to God, and the prisoners were listening to them, and suddenly there was a great earthquake, so that the foundations of the prison were shaken. And immediately all the doors were opened, and everyone's bonds were unfastened. When the jailer woke and saw that the prison doors were open, he drew his sword and was about to kill himself, supposing that the prisoners had escaped. But Paul cried with a loud voice, "Do not harm yourself, for we are all here." And the jailer called for lights and rushed in, and trembling with fear he fell down before Paul and Silas. Then he brought them out and said, "Sirs, what must I do to be saved?" And they said, "Believe in the Lord Jesus, and you will be saved, you and your household."

When you take the step to believe in your Heart that Jesus Christ is your Lord and Savior, you will be forgiven of all your sins and the Holy Spirit will replace Satan's demonic spirit in your heart.

In Romans 10:9–10, Paul wrote,

Because, if you *confess* with your mouth that Jesus is Lord and *believe in your heart* that God raised him from the dead, you will be saved. For with the heart one believes and is justified, and with the mouth one confesses and is saved. (Emphasis mine)

Jesus said in John 8:24

Unless you believe that I am He you will die in your sins. (Emphasis mine)

Chapter 25

Accepting Christ

What are we like before we accept Christ into our Heart? We are a sinner by nature. Sin will cause us to: Do things we never intended to do. Take us farther than we are willing to go. Cost us more than we are willing to pay. (Author unknown)

We are sinners by nature born with the sin nature in our hearts. We are on a pathway to hell. Matthew 7:13–14 reads,

Enter by the narrow gate. For the gate is wide and the way is easy that leads to destruction, and those who enter by it are many. For the gate is narrow and the way is hard that leads to life, and those who find it are few.

We have not yet accepted Christ into our hearts.

Thoughts about the Heart

- The heart is where I choose to do good or evil, to accept or reject Christ.
- It is the place where I say, "My will be done" or "God's will be done."
- It is the place where I am comfortable doing what I am doing and being who I am.
- It is the place where my mentor—either the Holy Spirit or Satan—dwells.
- It is where my conscience resides to judge my actions whether good or evil.

To be a true Christian, pray this prayer,

I believe that Jesus Christ is the Son of God who was born of the Virgin Mary and fathered by God's Holy Spirit.

I believe He shed His blood on a cruel cross and died as a ransom for my sins.

I believe He arose again from the dead on the third day and was witnessed by His disciples that He was alive.

I believe He ascended into heaven and sits at the right hand of the Father.

I believe He is coming again to claim me as His own.

I accept Him into my heart as my Savior.

If you prayed this prayer and accepted Him into your heart, He will come in and forgive you of all your sins

Today, I have accepted Christ as my Savior.

Signed_________________________________ Date______________

So what really happened to you?

First, you opened your heart and allowed Jesus Christ to enter and become your Redeemer. At this point, you are born again, and as such, you require only the milk of the Word as you are a babe in Christ. In 1 Corinthians 3:1–2, we read,

> "But I, brothers, could not address you as spiritual people, but as people of the flesh, as infants in Christ. I fed you with milk, not solid food, for you were not ready for it. And even now you are not yet ready."

Second, you received a deposit of the Holy Spirit to teach you, lead you, and help you grow in your new, born-again experience. The demonic spirit has been ejected from your heart; however, he will still try to tempt you from outside your heart. The Holy Spirit has come into your heart and you have become the temple of God. Paul asked in 1 Corinthians 3:16,

> "Do you not know that you are God's temple and that God's Spirit dwells in you?"

Third, you have allowed Christ into your life, but you are still in control of your heart. The Holy Spirit will gently lead you to turn over complete control of your heart to Him. When you do this, you set yourself apart to be used as the Holy Spirit directs.

Fourth, as the Holy Spirit leads you, you will begin to see changes for the better as the Holy Spirit will be doing some house cleaning by leading you to cast out the detrimental residents of your heart.

Appendix 1

Why I Believe in the God of the Bible

Science has now proven with certainty the beginning of the universe. Calling it for lack of a better term the big bang and that time, space, and matter had been compacted into something smaller than a pinhead; they call it nothingness.

On January 1, 2002, Dr. Hugh Ross, a noted astrophysicist who became a Christian because of the findings of science and a Gideon Bible, penned an article titled "Anthropic Principle: A Precise Plan for Humanity." This is an excerpt from that article.

In 1961, astronomers acknowledged just two characteristics of the universe as "fine-tuned" to make physical life possible.[1] The more obvious one was the ratio of the gravitational force constant to the electromagnetic force constant. It cannot differ from its value by any more than one part in 10^{40} (one part in ten thousand trillion trillion) without eliminating the possibility for life. Today, the number of known cosmic characteristics recognized as fine-tuned for life— any conceivable kind of physical life—stands at thirty-eight.[2] Of these, the most sensitive is the space energy density (the self-stretching property of the universe). Its value cannot vary by more than one part in 10^{120} and still allow for the kinds of stars and planets physical life requires.[3]

Evidence of specific preparation for human

existence shows up in the characteristics of the solar system as well. In the early 1960s astronomers could identify just a few solar system characteristics that required fine-tuning for human life to be possible. By the end of 2001, astronomers had identified more than 150 finely-tuned characteristics.[4] In the 1960s the odds that any given planet in the universe would possess the necessary conditions to support intelligent physical life were shown to be less than one in ten thousand.[5] In 2001 those odds shrank to less than one in a number so large it might as well be infinity (10^{173}).[6]

An account of scientific evidence in support of the anthropic principle fills several books.[7] the authors' religious beliefs run the gamut from agnosticism to deism to theism, but virtually every research astronomer alive today agrees that the universe manifests exquisite fine-tuning for life.[8]

(Here are the references Dr. Ross supplied for the above.

1. Robert H. Dicke, "Dirac's Cosmology and Mach's Principle," *Nature* 192 (1961), 440-41.

2. Hugh Ross, "Fine-Tuning for Life in the Universe," Appendix C, *Lights in the Sky and Little Green Men* (Colorado Springs, CO: NavPress, 2002), in press.

3. Lawrence M. Krauss, "The End of the Age Problem and the Case for a Cosmological Constant Revisited," *Astrophysical Journal* 501 (1998): 461-66.

4. Hugh Ross, "Probability for a Life Support Body,"

Appendix B, *Lights in the Sky and Little Green Men* (Colorado Springs, CO: NavPress, 2002), in press. It is also posted on the Reasons To Believe Web site at www.reasons.org.

5. I. S. Shklovskii and Carl Sagan, *Intelligent Life in the Universe* (San Francisco: Holden-Day, 1966), 342-61.

6. Ross, "Probability for a Life Support Body," Appendix B, *Lights in the Sky and Little Green Men.*

7. John D. Barrow and Frank J. Tipler, *The Anthropic Cosmological Principle* (New York: Oxford University Press, 1986); F. Bertola and U. Curi, eds., *The Anthropic Principle* (Cambridge: Cambridge University Press, 1993); Paul Davies, *The Cosmic Blueprint* (New York: Simon & Schuster, 1988); Michael J. Denton, *Nature's Destiny* (New York: The Free Press, 1998); George Greenstein, *The Symbiotic Universe* (New York: William Morrow, 1988); Hugh Ross, *The Creator and the Cosmos*, 3d ed.(Colorado Springs, CO: NavPress, 2001); Peter D. Ward and Donald Brownlee, *Rare Earth* (New York: Copernicus, 2000).

8. Quotes from nineteen astronomers who have done research on the anthropic principle may be found in Hugh Ross, *The Creator and the Cosmos*, 3d ed., 157–60.

See the complete article: "Anthropic Principle: A Precise Plan for Humanity" by Hugh Ross at: www.reasons.org

Science now claims that there are more than 850 "finely tuned characteristics required for life to appear anywhere in the Universe."

Science has "proven" that the universe had a beginning, and science universally agrees on a principal called cause and effect—nothing occurs without a cause. Christians agree that God was the cause of the universe coming into being; it didn't just happen without a cause!

If we can accept the proven facts of science that the universe was created and finely tuned for life, isn't it also probable that the God of creation also created man as stated in the Bible and as our Creator, He created us for a purpose and desires a relationship with us?

God's Plan for Your Life

The Bible tells us that it was God's plan that we live forever with Him in heaven. However, Satan interrupted God's plan and caused man to sin against God. This caused man to be separated from a relationship with his Creator. Sinning against God requires a punishment—death. When Adam and Eve sinned, they immediately died spiritually. God in His love and mercy sent His Son to pay the price of shedding His blood for our sins.

In John 3:14–17 (KJV), we read,

> And as Moses lifted up the serpent in the wilderness, even so, must the Son of man be lifted up: That whosoever believeth in him should not perish, but have eternal life. For God so loved the world, that he gave his only begotten Son, *that whosoever believeth in him should not perish, but have everlasting life.* For God sent not his Son into the world to condemn the world; but that the world through him might be saved. (Emphasis mine)

He died on a cross, rose again on the third day, and

ascended into heaven to be our Redeemer. Accept Him into your heart and you will be forgiven of your sins, resurrect your dead spiritual body, and receive eternal life. Without Him, you will not receive eternal life.

Appendix 2

Can We Trust the Bible?

Genesis 1:1 declares, "In the beginning God created the Heavens and the Earth"; that declares that God was in existence before the universe was created.

In Genesis, God reveals to us the events of His creative activities leading up to His creation of mankind. Science confirms that indeed the order of events revealed in the Bible is correct. The likelihood that man would guess the correct order of events is nigh unto impossible.

Over the years, science, which was at odds with biblical assertions concerning creative and historical information, has one by one admitted that the Bible got it right thousands of years before science found out the facts.

Biblical writers got it right because God revealed the truth to them; in reality, He is the author of the Bible. The writers simply recorded what God told them to write.

How else could Daniel predict over 500 years before Christ was born that 70 weeks were appointed for Israel beginning at a point when a decree would be given to restore and rebuild Jerusalem, each day of the week equaling one year? Following this decree, Christ would be cut off (crucified) after 69 weeks or 483 years. The crucifixion of Christ occurred on the exact day when the 483 years ended. Daniel 9:24–26 reads,

> Seventy weeks are decreed about your people and your holy city, to finish the transgression, to put an end to sin, and to

atone for iniquity, to bring in everlasting righteousness, to seal both vision and prophet, and to anoint a most holy place. Know therefore and understand that from the going out of the word to restore and build Jerusalem to the coming of an anointed one, a prince, there shall be seven weeks. Then for sixty-two weeks it shall be built again with squares and moat, but in a troubled time. And after the sixty-two weeks, an anointed one shall be cut off and shall have nothing. And the people of the prince who is to come shall destroy the city and the sanctuary. Its end shall come with a flood, and to the end there shall be war. Desolations are decreed.

What are the odds Daniel would know a decree would be given to rebuild Jerusalem and that the Messiah would be cut off 483 years after that decree? Very conservatively, 1 in a 1,000? It's more like 1 in 100,000 or more.

Approximately 500 years before Christ was born, Micah the prophet prophesied He would be born in Bethlehem of Judah; Micah 5:2 reads,

But you, O Bethlehem Ephrata, who are too little to be among the clans of Judah, from you shall come forth for me one who is to be ruler in Israel, whose coming forth is from of old, from ancient days.

What is this probability? Maybe 1 in 1,000 again, but let us be conservative and say 1 in 100, which is less than the available towns in Judah at that time.

Isaiah's prophecy was about a king named Cyrus who would destroy the mighty Babylonian empire and allow the exiled Jews to return to Jerusalem. This prophecy occurring some 150 years before Cyrus was even born and some 80 years before the Jews were defeated by the Babylonian Empire and taken into exile.

> Who says of Cyrus, "He is my shepherd, and he shall fulfill all my purpose"; saying of Jerusalem, "She shall be built," and of the temple, "Your foundation shall be laid." (Isaiah 4:28)

> Thus says the LORD to his anointed, to Cyrus, whose right hand I have grasped, to subdue nations before him and to loose the belts of kings, to open doors before him that gates may not be closed. (Isaiah 45:1)

> "I have stirred him up in righteousness, and I will make all his ways level; he shall build my city and set my exiles free, not for price or reward," says the LORD of hosts. (*Isaiah 45:13*)

Again, what was the probability of this prophecy coming true? Is it 1 in 10,000,000? Let us be extremely conservative and say 1 in 1,000.

Zechariah prophesied some 480 years before the time of Christ that He would be betrayed for thirty pieces of silver and that the money would purchase a potter's field for the burial of the poor. Zechariah 11:12–13 reads,

> Then I said to them, "If it seems good to you, give me my wages; but if not, keep them."

And they weighed out as my wages thirty pieces of silver. Then the LORD said to me, "Throw it to the potter"—the lordly price at which I was priced by them. So I took the thirty pieces of silver and threw them into the house of the LORD, to the potter.

The fulfillment of this was recorded in Matthew 26:14–15.

Then one of the twelve, whose name was Judas Iscariot, went to the chief priests and said, "What will you give me if I deliver him over to you?" And they paid him thirty pieces of silver.

Matthew 27:6–10 reads,

But the chief priests, taking the pieces of silver, said, "It is not lawful to put them into the treasury, since it is blood money." So they took counsel and bought with them the potter's field as a burial place for strangers. Therefore that field has been called the Field of Blood to this day.

Then was fulfilled what had been spoken by the prophet Jeremiah, saying, "And they took the thirty pieces of silver, the price of him on whom a price had been set by some of the sons of Israel, and they gave them for the potter's field, as the Lord directed me."

Again, what are the possibilities that Zechariah could have correctly prophesied this event? Maybe 1 in 10,000?

The probability that these four events predicted were fulfilled is 1 x 1,000 x 100 x 1,000 x 1,000, 1 chance in 100 billion.

There are at least sixty prophecies concerning Jesus in the Bible. If each prophecy had only 1 chance in 10 of being fulfilled, the odds of all sixty being fulfilled would be 1 in 10 followed by sixty zeros. Impossible!

Incidentally, all sixty were fulfilled.